This book is dedicated to the memory of my childhood librarian, Ms. Betty Worley, who died right as this book was about to publish. Without Ms. Betty, there would not be the me who loves to read and who has always dreamed of writing books. She instilled in me a love of reading and inspired me to challenge myself with difficult texts from a young age. She's the reason I wanted to be a librarian when I was younger (a dream never realized) and truly one of the finest people my town has ever known. I've been blessed to have many teachers and other influential figures that recognized a writing talent in me that I could dedicate this text to, but Ms. Betty, this one is for you.

INTRODUCTION

This collection is a compilation of hilarious things my children have said and done, which I often share on my social media. I have now decided to share these tales with a wider audience due to the widespread joy these stories seem to have brought my online followers. I am Ashley, married to a man also named Ashley, and together we have four children: Avery, Anson, Archer, and Ada. As of this publishing, all are under the age of nine. These comedic tidbits have been compiled in a Google Doc on my computer over the course of their existence. Since Archer and Ada are still quite young, and often incapable of the sort of hilarity their older brothers create, I feel confident this could be a multivolume series. I consider myself to be a fairly funny individual, and now that I have reproduced, I have learned that humor must be genetic—either that or the Lord has really blessed me with these accidental comedians who, as of yet, have no idea they're funny. I hope you enjoy their antics as much as their dad and I have (and, sometimes, we just laugh so we don't cry).

Here we are in all our glory—and, apparently, there are so many of us that the photographer had to sacrifice half of our oldest kid's face to snap this photo.

Thanks for purchasing, thanks for reading, and thanks to all who encouraged me to write this book.

With love, Ashley (October 2024)

My second-born son, waking me from a deep sleep at 5:45 a.m.:
Mama, how much do you know about farts?

◆ ◆ ◆

"WOW. This is the best meal I've ever had." -My oldest son
(who comes from a long line of incredible Southern cooks) at a Ft.
Payne, Alabama, Huddle House

◆ ◆ ◆

I guess driving dump trucks is rough work, even when the
dump truck is fake and you aren't actually driving anything.

◆ ◆ ◆

Overheard while I'm in the bathroom getting ready:
Anson: *I'm calling 911!!*
Me: runs out of the bathroom screaming, "No, don't do that!"

Then I realize he's "calling" 911 with a calculator.

My four-year-old once told me in the dead of August that there would be no school that day because "Jesus told me it was going to snow."

Avery: *Mom, do you know what to do during a bear attack?*
Me: *Um, lay really still?*
Avery: *No. You die. They use their claws to RIP. YOU. TO. SHREDS.*
Me: ....
Avery: *Anyway, can I get some apple juice?*

I worried during the pandemic that I was letting my oldest have too much YouTube screentime. This was pretty much confirmed when he asked me one day if we could have "prison burritos" for dinner, and he gave me step-by-step details on how to make them.

Enjoy this photo of my oldest from his third-grade yearbook (the year his school accidentally scheduled photo day and Wild West day on the same day).

◆ ◆ ◆

Anson, 8:04 a.m.: barfs all over hell and half of Georgia
Anson, 8:07 a.m.: *I want somethin' to eat.*

◆ ◆ ◆

Avery: *How many pounds are you?*

Me: *I don't want to say.* (I don't need him telling all his buddies how much his mama weighs. What if they make it a competition and he wins?!)

Avery: *I'm going to guess, then. Is it 1,000 pounds?*

Me: *NOOOO.*

Avery: *OK, then. Higher or lower?*

My view at every meal: They're either begging for it or sneezing near it.

Avery: *Krakens are like big octupuses and they eat chips.*

Me: *I think you mean "ships."*

Avery: *No, they eat chips. … Like Ruffles.*

When my son was given this "53" placard at a restaurant after we ordered our food, he thought it meant he would get 53 ice creams. IMAGINE THE DISAPPOINTMENT!

Upon losing his first tooth:
Me: *How much money do you think the Tooth Fairy will leave you?*
Avery: *Probably $1,000.*

Avery: *I prayed to Jesus for patience and understanding. And also that Anson wouldn't get anything for Christmas.*

Avery, introducing my mom to one of his friends from preschool: *This is Rosa Lee. She's my grandma. She has white hair and she wears panties.* (This is probably my favorite funny thing Avery has said to date.)

◆ ◆ ◆

My oldest son once asked me if I was older than Bob Barker.

◆ ◆ ◆

I snapped this photo of my youngest son on vacation enjoying spaghetti, his favorite food. An hour later, he threw up this spaghetti in the hotel pool, which had to be evacuated and closed for cleaning.

◆ ◆ ◆

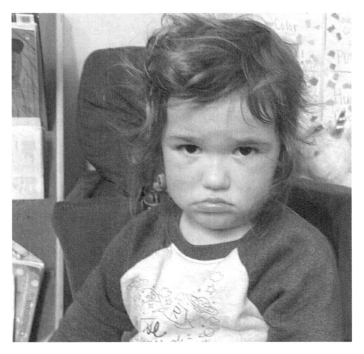

The look I got when I had the *audacity* to take the last bite of my own yogurt.

◆ ◆ ◆

Woman at the store to Avery: *How old are you?*
Avery, without hesitation: *40.*
(He was two and a half.)

◆ ◆ ◆

One morning as we were rushing to the car—there is no other way to get to the car except by rushing when you have children—Anson said, "Mommy, don't forget your pants!" And he said it so convincingly that I panicked for a nanosecond. I checked to make sure I was actually wearing pants (I was). Then he laughed at me all the way to school.

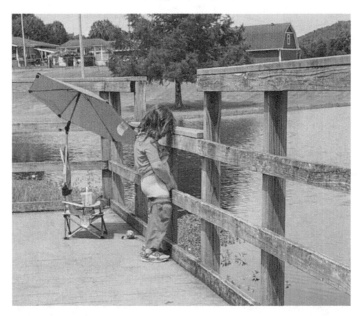

As the mother of three boys, I can confidently say they fall into one of two categories: will only pee in bathrooms that have passed CDC inspections or will pee anywhere in front of anyone (I have one of the former and two of the latter).

❖ ❖ ❖

Avery asked, "MOM. What's that on your eyes?!"
I replied, "Makeup."
And Avery said, "Oh. It looks ... pretty. I guess." [pause] "Yeah. I ... guess."

❖ ❖ ❖

Me: *Love you, Avery.*
Avery: *Love you too.* [pause] *Love Daddy more, though.*
I mean ... I gave you life and Daddy won't even share his popcorn with you, but OK.

❖ ❖ ❖

My little vacation Bible school dropout. This was taken at my mom's church's VBS. I think my kids are the reason that her church no longer offer VBS.

Avery: *MOM, ANSON KICKED ME!*
Me: *He is just playing. He wasn't trying to be malicious.*
Avery: *HE WAS TOO TRYING TO BE DELICIOUS.*

Avery found a flash drive under the seat of my car once and asked accusingly if it was drug paraphernalia.

When my oldest was about three, I took him to McDonald's for a Happy Meal. But when we got there, he cried and loudly asked, in front of everyone, if we could go home so he could eat the Happy Meal off his POO PLATE. He meant his Winnie-the-Pooh plate, but try explaining that to all the horrified onlookers.

When we went in for our first ultrasound with Ada, the doctor said, "Wow. Four kids! How many kids do you guys want?" And since it's always best to be honest with your doctor, my husband said, "Two."

Last Mother's Day, Avery asked me how I felt when World War II ended, so, in other words, he sure knows how to make a mom feel loved on her special day.

One Sunday, Ada needed a new diaper during church, so my husband got up to take her out just before the sermon started. Our two-year-old followed; then our four-year-old went with them, too. Upon seeing that, four or five other children from the church followed my husband out, thinking he was leading a children's church parade. What started as a quick diaper change ended up as my husband babysitting about eight kids for the duration of the service.

When the photographer just gives up on getting a good shot and sends you this one of your kid picking his nose. Like I don't have a dozen of these already.

Avery, painting a birdhouse.
Me: *Why did you paint the number "10" on the side?*
Avery: *That's how many years I've been painting birdhouses.*
Me: *You're seven.*

On the way to school one morning, Avery asked me what "dying" really means, so I stuttered and stammered through an explanation that I'm sure he'll tell his therapist all about one day. When I got through, he looked at me in horror and said, "No, I meant the other kind of dyeing. Like Easter eggs."

◆ ◆ ◆

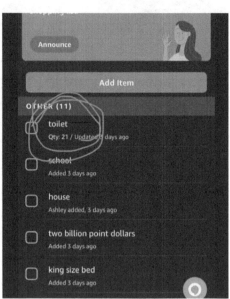

Lord help you when your kids figure out how to add things to the shopping list via Alexa. Twenty-one toilets?!

I once placed a McDonald's order for Avery, and I asked Anson if he wanted a hamburger. He said no, so I didn't get him anything. But then when he saw Avery with a McDonald's bag, he got mad.

I said, "You said you didn't want a hamburger!"

And Anson said, "BECAUSE I WANTED TWO HAMBURGERS."

◆ ◆ ◆

Me to Avery: *Anson had a bad day at daycare. He got choked.*

Avery: *Who choked him?!?*

Me: *Nobody! He choked on his food.*

Avery: *Oh. I figured somebody finally got tired of him and choked him.*

One of the biggest meltdowns my house has ever seen was when I tried to pass Aldi-brand 'Doritos' off as the real deal.

When I found out I was pregnant with our second child, I worried I couldn't love another one as much as I loved the first. But now that I have four, I know there's no such thing as having a favorite. I dislike them all equally most days.

Avery: *Mom, when I turn 18, will you help me apply for a credit card? If you're still alive?*

My town has a huge parade on the Fourth of July that the whole town watches. One year, I had to take the kids alone because my husband had to work, so I put Anson on a leash. Here's how that worked out.

We always give the kids some money to put in the offering plate at church, but I forgot both cash and check one Sunday. When Avery realized I didn't have anything for the offering, his eyes got wide with horror. He said, "Oh no. Are we going to get in trouble?!"

Avery: sneezes
Me: *Bless you!*
Avery: *I'm so glad you said that.* [pause] *Because you did NOT when I sneezed last Wednesday.*

Avery: *Anson, hush! I need some shut-eye.*
Anson: *Too bad! I want some … open-eye?*

It is mind-blowing how much damage one Pop-Tart can do to a living room in the hands of a ruthless toddler. It would be easier to get new furniture than to find all the errant crumbs and brown sugar cinnamon smears.

"Mama, how would you kill a Bigfoot? Like a Bazooka would probably do it, right?" These are the kinds of questions you get to try to stammer an answer to regularly as a parent.

No matter how hard you try, sometimes a Happy Meal is just an "I Hate My Life Meal."

Then there was a time we were in Walmart. It was close to Christmas and jam-packed, and Avery (age two) started screaming, "CHICKEN BALLS! CHICKEN BALLS!" He meant that he wanted popcorn chicken from the Walmart deli for dinner, but that's not information the crowd of disgusted onlookers had.

Avery: *Where's Daddy?*
Me: *He ran to the drugstore.*
Avery, visibly panicking: *OH MY GODDDDDD, MY DADDY DOES DRUGS?!*

Avery is so much like his dad it usually feels like he got nothing from me, but I once heard him whisper, "I love you" to his potato chips and thought, "Ahhh there I am, after all."

Me: *Kids, I have to finish this project like NOW. Please please please, just be calm and chill, and watch TV and play with your toys for 15*

minutes.

My kids: got a balloon stuck in the ceiling fan

Me: eating my lunch, minding my business
Avery, shoving his hands in my face: *MOM, SMELL MY HANDS! THEY SMELL JUST LIKE WET DOG!*

In the time it took me to carry a bag of groceries into the house, Anson, at eighteen months old, managed to ascend his father's motorcycle.

My husband: *Anson, do you want a new baby sister?*
Anson: *No, I want a hamburger.*

Employee at McDonald's: *Thanks, have a nice day!*
Anson: *SHUT UPPPPPPP!*

◆ ◆ ◆

When we go to yard sales, I always give the kids a few bucks to spend. That's how we came to be the owners of this one-eyed duck pen that doesn't write.

Parenting is HARD. Try explaining to a two-year-old why a horse says neigh neigh but a seahorse does not say neigh neigh.

Us: *What do you want for Christmas this year, Anson?*
Anson: *Some Play-doh. $100,000 dollars.*

Looking at a pair of pajamas that he's worn 100 times very

intently, Anson said, "My God, this shirt has SLEEVES!"

◆ ◆ ◆

Check out this giant door prize my kid once won at VBS (six-year-old for scale). This thing lived in my living room for three months before we convinced him to let us move it to his bedroom. It took up a quarter of his room for another year before he finally agreed to let us get rid of it to make room for a Christmas tree. RIP, Ramsey.

The unbridled joy our daughter felt while looking at this Halloween skeleton display was only *slightly* alarming.

Avery: *OWWW Anson, why did you hit me?? That hurt!*
Anson: *It felt good to me!*

Once when I was putting Anson in his car seat, Avery walked around to the other side of the car parallel to the road. When I got through with Anson and rounded the corner to put Avery in the car, HE WAS STANDING ON THE SIDEWALK WITH HIS THUMB OUT TRYING TO HITCHHIKE.

Archer: *Mama, I farted.*
Me: ignores him because someone is always farting
Archer: *It's on the carpet.*
("Farts," vomit, and the like on the carpet always conveniently seem to happen when Dad is at work.)

I once went into a bakery with the kids and told them each they could have ONE THING. Anson goes up to the counter and said, "I will have one cake, please."

Avery: *Who was Shakespeare?*
Me: *One of the greatest writers who ever lived.*
Avery: *Were y'all friends?*

Once when Avery and Anson were arguing about something, Anson told Avery, "This town ain't big enough for the two of us."

She's fine; she just dropped her french fry and couldn't find it, thus experiencing what was, to date, the worst day of her life.

Anson and Archer were playing hide and seek. Archer WATCHED Anson hide. Then he counted to 20, looked all over the house, and started crying because he couldn't find Anson. (I really hoped to have a child prodigy, but it was not meant to be.)

This meltdown was brought on because I wouldn't buy him a bottle of wine at the grocery store. I almost bought myself one, though.

I once put the incorrect amount of butter on Anson's breakfast, and he looked me dead in the eyes and said, "I am so disappointed in you."

When you normalize waist-down nudity at home while potty training your two-year-old, there is a chance he may enjoy it so much, even after potty training, that he strips his pants and underwear off and runs to the front of the church in the middle of the sermon. There is also a chance that, on a separate occasion, he runs to the neighbors' house (while they have company) and into their back door and right onto their expensive white couch while wearing nothing but a T-shirt. Ask me how I know.

Once while Daddy was at work, Ada desperately needed a nap. I turned the TV on for the boys, and we went in the next room to lay down (she won't sleep alone). I told them not to enter the room (she's a light sleeper) unless there was an emergency. But of course, there WAS an emergency, which was that Anson couldn't open his Gogurt by himself.

Avery to his brother while playing: *Are you thinkin' what I'm thinkin'?*

Anson: *Yep!* [pause] *I'm thinkin' 'bout cheese!*

Me: *Anson, HOW. MANY. TIMES. do I have to ask you not to do that?*

Anson, while doing it anyway: *Prolly at least six.*

"No, Mommy. I not eat all the powdered donuts." So that's just cocaine on your face, then?

Once when I was alone in a room with Avery (he was about four), he said, "Are you all right?"
And I answered, "Yes."
And Avery said, "I WAS TALKING TO MYSELF."

One day when I picked Anson up from daycare and was buckling him in the car, we could hear the sounds of the other kids playing outside.
Anson: *All my friends are playing on the playground.* [pauses, lowers his voice] *And so are my enemies.*

One Christmas season, Anson (age three) constantly sang "Santa Claus Is Coming to Town," but he thought the lyrics were, "You better not pout! You better not die!" (which is probably not an entirely inaccurate warning about how best to enjoy the season).

◆ ◆ ◆

My mother had a coughing fit one morning when Avery was about three years old. She coughed and coughed, and Avery grew very concerned. He asked, "Grandma! Are you OK?" And she said, "Yes, I'm fine. I just have a frog in my throat." So Avery crawled into her lap and said, "That is SO GROSS. Lemme see the frog!"

◆ ◆ ◆

My children went through a phase where the youngest boy would pee in the driveway, and the two older boys would try to figure out what shape it was in, like some sort of urine divination.

Anson was sitting criss-cross applesauce at the kitchen table eating nacho cheese and tortilla chips. Having dripped some cheese on the side of his foot, he used a tortilla chip to scrape it off. Not satisfied with those results, he proceeded to lick his foot clean, the same way a cat would do.

❖ ❖ ❖

Our oldest went through a phase where he wouldn't go to church without grabbing a toy, and it was usually something wildly inappropriate like a hula hoop (top) or a beach ball larger than him (bottom).

❖ ❖ ❖

Once, right after my two-year-old figured out how to take a photo with a smartphone, he ran into the bathroom, took a photo of me on the toilet, and tore back out of the bathroom giggling all the way.

❖ ❖ ❖

One Saturday morning, I was home alone with four kids, and we were watching "Mickey Mouse Clubhouse." Anson kept asking for something to eat, but I couldn't get up because Ada was asleep on me (and don't feel sorry for him, he'd already had breakfast). Anyway, Minnie Mouse was explaining fractions and she cut a pie into six pieces. Anson looked me dead in the eyes and said, "Wish I had six pieces of pie." Yeah, well, me too, buddy.

One day, Anson asked me how old his dad was, and I said, "42." (He was actually 41 at this time and I just gave the wrong age mistakenly!) Anson's mouth fell open and he said, "WOW. [pause] OK. That ... surely is a lot of years."

My children's energy is always endless at home. But 10 minutes into their $50, hourlong jump at the trampoline park, they proclaimed: "We're tired."

When I was trying to teach Avery his colors, age two:
Me, handing Avery a yellow M&M: *What color is this, Avery?*
Avery: *Cat!*

Avery once burst into tears because he waved at a horse we drove past, and it didn't wave back.

Archer: babbles like a toddler (because he's a toddler)
Avery: COME SAY IT TO MY FACE LIKE A MAN!

During the 2024 summer Olympics, Avery (age eight) asked me —the most uncoordinated, ungraceful, unathletic person to ever walk (stumble, really) across this planet— if I had ever competed in the Olympics.

Avery: *Mom, how big is my room?*
Me: *Um, maybe like 12 or 14 feet?*
Avery: *Yeah, but that's adult feet. How many kid feet?*

Avery: *Who was your kindergarten teacher, Mom?*
Me: *A lady named Ms. Eberhart. I don't know if she still teaches or what she's doing now.*
Avery: *Oh, I doubt it. She's probably dead.*

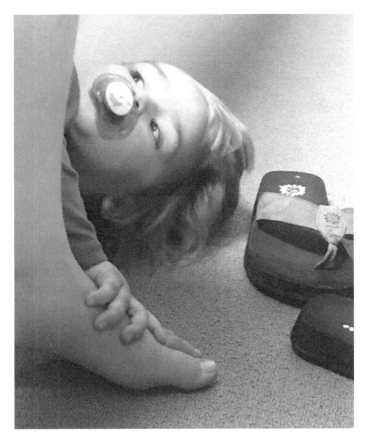

There was a time that my oldest son had a severe foot fetish —he would crawl under pews at church, remove folks' shoes, and play with their toes. It was both disgusting and worrisome. I am ashamed to admit I let him do it so that he would let me enjoy church in peace. I am also very happy to report he seems to have outgrown it.

I once had a *bathroom emergency* and had to ask my husband to pull into the nearest fast-food restaurant. That was over a year ago, and we have never passed that restaurant again without my middle son saying, "THAT'S WHERE MOMMY HAD TO POOP THAT TIME."

◆ ◆ ◆

Here's another gem from yearbook picture day/Wild West day. It's a crying shame his hat didn't make it in.

When Avery was in second grade, they did a unit on birds, which filled him with interesting bird facts about flamingo feather pigmentation and robin migration patterns. One day he came home during this period and said, "Mama, did you know hummingbirds are bossy? JUST LIKE YOU!"

Once when he was very small, Avery started whining in the backseat of the car and asked for a potty. The closest bathroom available for the public I could think of was a Kohl's. I got there, got him out of the car, and rushed him toward the sliding glass doors —and he projectile vomited alllllll over those glass doors before they could even detect our movement and open. But then, they *did* detect our movement and open, smearing the mess inside the doors as well. I stood there in horror. I had no idea what to do. I ran back to the car for something to clean with, but all I had were a few baby wipes. I ended up telling an employee, who got the assistant manager, who got the manager—who had to lock the doors, get out their squeegee, and stop all traffic in and out of the store while she cleaned it up. I just stood there because she wouldn't let me help, but it seemed rude to just bolt. When she finished, I managed an awkward, "OK, thanks. Bye!" before going back to my car to be humiliated in private.

When Avery was at the age where he was learning lots of new vocabulary, he learned the words "bull" and "ghost" in the same day. The result was that he often mixed them up. So he'd say things like "Our house is full of bulls for Halloween!" and "That ghost has big horns!" But one night in October, as I was driving at dusk down a lonely road, he screamed, "LOOK, MOM, THERE'S A GHOST!" after seeing a bull. I nearly put the car in a ditch.

Daycare must have been rough on this day. Anson's teacher sent me this photo of him looking like he was at the bar on his third whiskey neat while an Alan Jackson song played on the jukebox.

Before I had children, I had no idea I could ruin a kid's day by putting ketchup on the right side of a plate instead of the left. But now I know I can ruin the kid's day, my own day, the neighbor's day, and our mailman's day if I'm not careful and deliberate with condiment placement.

My oldest went through a time where he wanted to be a singer when he grew up—Michael Jackson, mostly. Having no talent in the vocal or dance department, he was always notoriously two beats behind the music. My husband described him as "the Internet Explorer of kid singers." But enjoy this picture of him dressed as "Smooth Criminal" MJ for career day.

When my husband went by the daycare to pick up an application to enroll our second child, they misunderstood what he wanted and handed him an application for employment instead. He was 10 or so questions into the application when he got home before he realized there had been a terrible mistake.

I know some parents get annoyed when people imply that having dogs is similar to having children. But when Avery was little, he would stand in front of the fridge and beg for a piece of cheese before bedtime every night, so I personally don't think dogs and kids are all that different. It's just a shame that it's not socially acceptable to leave kids home and go on vacation without them.

I once, and only once, made the mistake of trying to take a shower while home alone with three kids. I hadn't been in the water for five seconds when I heard a giant crash upstairs. All three of their lives flashed before my eyes. I ran upstairs dripping bath water all the way. Anson had knocked over a shelf, scattering toys everywhere, but no one was injured, so I returned to the shower, leaving a second trail of water through the house. With my hair all shampooed up and my eyes closed, I heard the curtain open. Apparently, my phone had made a sound, and Anson—being the "good" little helper he is—decided to bring it to me. He threw it directly under the water, but somehow I caught it with one eye half-open and slung it back out of the shower in an effort to keep it dry, spraying water all over the bathroom once again, and shouted, "Noooo, Anson!!" He thought he was in trouble when I yelled at him, so he turned to run away—but there was so much water on the floor by then that he fell FOUR times while trying to make his getaway, crying louder each time he went down. His clothes got so sopping wet I had to change them. Then, I had to mop most of the house. I have not showered since when my husband isn't home.

If a child sees an opportunity to lift your dress up and show your underwear in public, they will take it. If parenting has taught me anything, it's this.

My kids once overheard a lady say, "Bitch, please!" at the grocery store, and I could tell by the way they looked at me they'd be using that phrase later. I was right, but luckily they misheard or misremembered it. Instead, they walked around saying, "Fish, cheese!" for a few days until the thrill wore off.

"Guys, we cannot bring guns to school": This is a talk my husband had with the kids as he was loading them in the car one morning. He was talking about Nerf guns, but I'm sure any neighbors who overheard were concerned at both the fact that elementary school students were armed—and my husband's lackadaisical response to his children packing heat.

Then there was the year that Anson refused to wear pants to Christmas play practice.

Here's how the play ultimately went (not great, in other words).

We once had a massive snowstorm and were snowed in with all four children for a week. By the fifth day, the daycare staff had decided to reopen, but we still couldn't get the car out of the driveway. I had made up my mind to carry the four-year-old and two-year-old on my back through ice and snow for more than three miles, just to be away from them for a little while. Then, my husband finally, and mercifully, got the car unstuck. He spent the rest of his day trying to determine the feasibility of a business that picks your kids up by drone and takes them to daycare, no matter the weather conditions.

♦ ♦ ♦

Anson: *Mom, farts are brown.*

♦ ♦ ♦

One year, I had already threatened a call to Santa by 7 a.m. on November 1, before the Halloween costumes had even been washed and returned to the closet.

Anson: *Mommy, I want a chocolate nonut!* [he meant donut]
Me: *No. You've been so bad at daycare the past few days.*
Anson: *MOMMY, I WANT A CHOCOLATE NONUT!*
Me: *NOOO.*
Anson: [pause] *I need to talk to Poppy.*
This is how three-year-olds ask for a manager.

If you've ever wondered what it's like to medicate a strong-bodied, strong-willed three-year-old, just know my Apple Watch registers it as exercise.

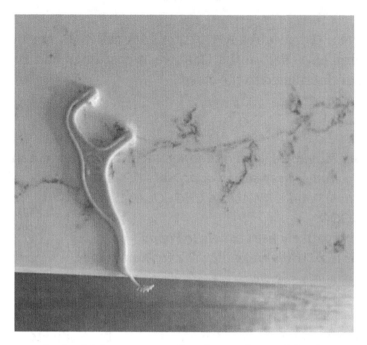

I once took the kids to a parade where they picked up candy off the ground. When we got home, I went through their candy and discovered they had also picked up someone's used dental flosser.

I once took Avery to the park when he was two. Another kid and his dad were there, and the other kid's nana showed up. The dad said (to his own kid, obviously): "Show Nana how good you can slide!" Avery pushed past the other kid at 100 mph to beat him to the slide and show "Nana" his sliding prowess. (Huge thanks to that nana for pretending she cared how well Avery could go down a slide.)

Anson: *Sharing is nice! Course I don't do it because I'm not nice. But you should.* [advice given to his little brother]

We often tried to use a leash on our unruly second child, and although I've trained many a dog to walk on a leash, I never could get my two-year-old to successfully do it.

My husband, talking to me about the McDonald's app: "My app is really buggy."

Anson, listening from the backseat: "Dad, your ass is really buggy?"

Avery, flipping me the bird: *Mom, I know what this means. It means "peace."*

We were driving through the middle of nowhere once on our way to vacation when Anson, who was only recently potty trained, had to go. The only bathroom we could find under his time constraints was absolutely filthy, but desperate times, desperate measures. After he finished going and I got his pants back on him, I turned around after unlocking the door to see him KISSING THE NASTIEST PUBLIC TOILET I HAD EVER LAID EYES ON. I considered leaving him there for another family to find.

◆ ◆ ◆

Avery: *Mom, do you know how much Godzilla eggs weigh?*
Me: *No.*
Avery: *1,000 pounds!* [slight pause] *Same as you!*

◆ ◆ ◆

We were once in a fender-bender in a residential neighborhood with a woman who clearly had addiction issues. Her neighbors were very upset that she had caused a wreck and came out in droves to tell her what they thought of her, which included the word "crackwhore." This, of course, prompted my children to inquire, "Mom, what's a crackwhore?" as I shushed them and begged them to stop repeating the word and asking me what it meant. I can't tell you how hard I prayed for them to not ask someone else this question, or use this phrase at church or school.

◆ ◆ ◆

Me: *Alexa, turn the bedroom light on.*
Alexa: [doesn't respond]
Anson: *ALEXA, I HAVE TO LISTEN TO MOMMY AND SO. DO. YOU.*

◆ ◆ ◆

I went to a little presentation on flowers/butterflies at Avery's elementary school one morning. Avery begged to leave when it was over. All his friends were leaving, so I was like, "OK, fine. But I have a LOT to do today, so I need you to be quiet and entertain yourself." He swore he would. But next thing I know, as I'm trying to work: "MOM! Let me sing you the pollination song we learned at school. It has four verses. HERE I GO." And then he proceeded to start over every time I broke eye contact.

Avery: *Mom, we wrote letters to Santa at school today, but I couldn't tell him everything I want because I don't know how to spell "Iwo Jima."*

Me: *... What, exactly, are you trying to ask Santa for?!?*

I made the kids hot dogs for dinner one night because I was just too exhausted to do anything else. I put ketchup on Anson's because he loves ketchup on his hot dogs. He cried because there was ketchup on it. I made him another and did not put ketchup on it. He cried because there was no ketchup. And then I no longer cared how hungry he was, he didn't get another hot dog.

Me: *DO NOT spray the hose in the garage. We don't need this cement floor getting all wet.*

Avery (age three): *Why? Are you afraid you'll bust your ass?*

Me: *DON'T SAY THAT. But also, yes. Mommy is definitely at the age where a broken hip is a major concern of hers.*

I took the oldest two (back when they were the only two) to a wedding once by myself (husband was working). The youngest was about 18 months old. During the ceremony, he gagged loudly, and I reacted the only way I knew how—by sticking my hands out to catch whatever was about to happen so that it didn't hit the lovely chairs or splatter loudly onto the floor. Thankfully, there wasn't a lot of it and I was able to catch it in my hands—but now what to do with my handful of vomit? I remembered seeing a bathroom at the front of the venue, so I started heading that way, my high heels loudly clickity-clacking against the venue's floors, causing even more of a scene. I had left my oldest (age five) behind thinking he would sit there nicely while I washed my hands, but no, he shouted, "MOMMY, DON'T LEAVE ME" and tore out of the room after me, prompting all eyes at the wedding to turn to look at us instead of the bride and groom. I figured the worst was over and decided to stay for the reception, but no, he gagged again, and I spilled sweet tea everywhere reacting to the sound.

Avery once made this D-Day memorial out of Legos, complete with the date written on the cross and some mini figures entombed inside the base. I didn't know then, and still don't know now, if this was heartwarming or terrifying.

Until having children, I never imagined a day could be ruined by an Easter egg. One Easter Sunday, however, my kid flushed one down the toilet. The day was indeed ruined, as was my outfit, a slew of towels, and possibly the toilet, which had to be replaced not long after.

One day, we went to an event where all kinds of kid-friendly foods were served, but Anson wouldn't eat anything. When we got home, I made him a grilled cheese, and he wouldn't eat that, either, so my husband and I said, "Sorry, kid. No more options." He balled up his little fists and got so mad that he stuttered and stammered as he tried to think of an insult that would hurt us. He finally said, "MOM, DAD, I HOPE YOU FART EVERY DAY."

Questions I was once asked in a 20-minute timeframe by my kids:
 -"How many pounds does our house weigh?"
 -"Did Jesus ever say bad words?"
 -"Does James's mom know who Godzilla is?" [I verified that she does.]
 -"Could Jesus see rocks good?"
 -"How many days until Halloween?" [It was March.]
 -"How do they make paper towels?"

Have you ever seen someone look so sad and dejected while being handed FREE CANDY on Halloween? (In his earliest years, Anson didn't like Halloween or Easter because they took "too much work.")

◆ ◆ ◆

During the COVID shutdown, Avery (age four) was having a snack of potato chips, which I was allowing because I was desperate to get anything done. He dropped one. Rather than pick it up, he STEPPED ON IT, grinding it into a million pieces. Obviously, he got in trouble (and lost his potato chip privileges). So the next morning, we had a little chat.

Me: *Are you gonna be a better boy today? You're not gonna drop food on the floor and step on it again, are you?*

Avery: [long pause] *I don't know. I might.*

Avery (age four): *Oh, s&$@!!*
Me: *AVERY. DO NOT SAY THAT. IT'S UGLY!*
Avery: *No, Mommy, you're ugly!*

My mom, who is in her 80s, has an ATV she uses to get around her property. Once while riding it with Avery, she got off to move something out of the way and fell down.
    Avery: *Grandma! Are you OK? Do you need an ambulance?*
    Mom: *No, I don't think so.*
    Avery: *Oh, OK. You going to meet Jesus, then?*

Archer went through a (thankfully brief) period where he called cupcakes "KKs," which sometimes came out of his mouth as "KKKs." I was SO WORRIED he'd say something in public about "loving KKKs."

Archer also went through a brief time were he called his jammies his "grammies." "Where are my grammies?" You don't have any, kid; you can't sing.

Me: *Avery, get out of the tub. I need a bath, too.*
Avery (age two): *Sorry, Mommy. I need a bath, one.*

One morning, Anson was singing "I'm in the Lord's Army" and Archer was trying to sing along. Anson said, "Bro, just STOP. You're not EVEN IN the Lord's army."

One of the really unpleasant parts of parenting is dealing with constipation. Ada and Archer both struggled with it, to the point that there was a time we were ordering suppositories in bulk on Amazon. (I was afraid to buy them in person, because heaven forbid one of my kids have a reason to say something about "Mommy shoving things up my butt" at the store.) Once my husband and I were doing a suppository assembly line, holding them down, trying to insert one. Everyone was thrashing and crying, as any child would. We were smackdab in the middle of this process, I'm talking legs in the air and butt cheeks spread, when Anson ran in the room with a book and says, "MOMMY, CAN YOU READ ME THIS STORY RIGHT NOW?"

My kids enjoy making each other cry by telling one another that Jesus doesn't love them anymore.

I tried to take a picture of my beautiful baby boy, but he spit up right as I did it, so what I got was this, like some horrifying baby Slipknot-esque album cover.

I once lost Anson (age two) at home. I had been putting away laundry and came back out of the closet to see he was nowhere to be found. I checked every room, under every bed, nothing. I went outside, looking up and down the immediate area, and again saw nothing. I was on my way back into the house to call my neighbors to see if he had shown up there (and if not, the police) when I heard the dryer giggle.

◆ ◆ ◆

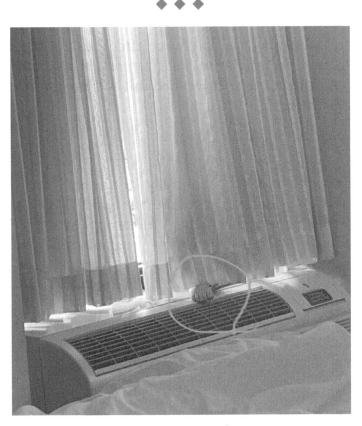

On a different occasion, I lost Anson while we were in a hotel room. Everyone was napping except me, and I got up to use the bathroom. When I came back, he was nowhere to be found. I didn't think he could've opened the door to the room by himself, and certainly not without me hearing it, but where could he have gone? I finally saw some chunky toes sticking out from under the curtains.

◆ ◆ ◆

Avery: *Mom, what was it like during that big flood?*

Me: *Which big flood? I've seen several floods in my lifetime.*
Avery: *The real big one. You know, the one Noah built the ark for.*

On the first Sunday back at church after the COVID quarantine shutdown, four-year-old Avery told everyone in his Sunday school class to keep him in their prayers because he'd been in the hospital [absolutely not true].

I kept Anson out of school one day for an appointment. When it was over, he was eager to get home, but I said, "I just have to run into this store for one quick thing." And he looked at me like I was full of it and said, "I didn't even know you could run."

I was at church working on a project in the fellowship hall and Anson said, "This is the room we eat in." And I said, "Yes, that's right." And he said, "OK, so why aren't we eating?"

In this photo, Anson is crying because the peanut butter jar is empty (he's the one who emptied it). He cried himself to sleep this night, clutching the jar, and woke up the next morning STILL crying. Needless to say, our first stop of the day was the peanut butter aisle at the grocery store.

Ash bought the kids a Wii at a yard sale, and Anson kept calling it a "weedeater." I had to tell my friends and family that if he told them we were letting him play with a weedeater to not be alarmed.

Anson and Avery drive Alexa crazy asking her random trivia and to play certain songs ("I Like to Move It, Move It" mostly), but poor Archer can't quite figure out what she's capable of and what she isn't. I once heard him say, "Alexa, why didn't Poppy come over today?"

◆ ◆ ◆

I don't know what's going on in this picture. Surely it's not five adults (myself *not included*—I was in favor of leaving them in there to think about what they'd done) trying to rescue two of my children from a room they accidentally locked themselves into at church. After 45 minutes of trying, and my kids growing increasingly panicked, the door ultimately had to be broken down. Doesn't close right to this day.

◆ ◆ ◆

Once when on vacation, we bought trolley tickets to make getting around easier. Sometimes when we'd board, there wouldn't be enough seats for us to all sit together. When this happened, the two oldest boys would have to go sit with strangers. On one such occasion, I overheard Anson, being oh so good at making friends, immediately and loudly tell the woman he sat next to that he had "pizza diarrhea" (a phrase I had never heard him use until that moment).

Avery: *Hey Mom. I know it's bad to put your middle finger up. BUT what about your middle toe?*

One time, my mom was making pork chops, and Avery didn't care for the odor. He said, "Ew, Grandma! What is that smell!?" She decided to mess with him and replied, "I'm making tongues for dinner." Obviously, she meant something like beef tongues that folks actually eat, but Avery, who had not eaten anything but nachos and french fries for roughly two years, had no concept of people eating any sort of tongue. He thought she meant human tongues and was *horrified.*

Avery, shouting across a crowded beach: *HEY MOM, I JUST FARTED IN THE WATER! HAVE YOU EVER FARTED IN WATER?!?*
Everyone on the beach: turns to look at me for my answer

When Anson was four, he started asking lots of questions about how babies get here. Avery told him they cut Ada out of my belly, and that really rocked him. So he asked me how Archer got here, and I said they cut him out, same as Ada. And then he said, "Did they cut me out, too?" And I said yep. And then he stared at me in disbelief and said, "Mom, you have GOT TO STOP eating babies."

As I was pulling out of the driveway with the kids one morning, I rolled down the window and said, "Y'all say bye to Daddy!" And Anson (age four) yelled, "Bye, loser!"

The Hall family: goes to a nice multi-family yard sale
Anson: drops his pants and pees in front of the "multi-family"

I am a huge advocate of volunteer work and do lots of such projects, which my kids are used to. After finishing up a community service project for foster kids, Avery had a lot of questions about what fostering means, etc. I guess he had foster kids on his mind as a result. Later, we were leaving Walmart and some middle school-age kids were selling snacks as a fundraiser for their sports teams. I gave Avery a few bucks to donate to them. As he walked away, he yelled, "Good luck, foster kids!"

Sunday school teacher: *Who likes to eat at restaurants?*
Anson, who is generally nonparticipatory at church: raises both hands and jumps to his feet

My boys are spoiled. I get them a donut almost every morning. One morning, I didn't have time because we had to be in the next city over for an early doctor's appointment. As you can imagine,

Anson, my little food lover, didn't handle this news well. While on the highway, we saw several police cars with lights flashing. Of course, the boys wanted to know what the issue was, but whatever it was was already cleared up, so I told them I didn't know. And Anson said, "Maybe they chased down a bad guy who didn't buy his kids donuts."

◆ ◆ ◆

What I said: *Come on in the house, kids!*
What my kids heard: *HIT EACH OTHER AS HARD AS YOU CAN WITH THOSE STICKS.*

◆ ◆ ◆

This meltdown of Anson's was brought on because I wouldn't let him eat a sticky, glazed, cream-filled donut in the car. We only had a four-minute drive ahead of us, but his fear of wasting away during that time was very real.

❖ ❖ ❖

I took Anson to a community event that had a waterslide inflatable shortly after finishing potty training. Imagine my *horror* when he came down the slide smearing brown stuff all the way, and my *relief* upon learning it was just mud.

❖ ❖ ❖

You know that phrase about swinging from chandeliers? Some children will literally try it. They're usually the same children who'd rather play in the road than on the playground.

Anson and Archer once argued ALL morning about whose "lucky day" it was (a phrase they didn't understand but heard from Avery). I can tell you with confidence whose lucky day it *was not*.

Preacher: pauses for a moment during his message
Anson: *MOMMY HAS A BIG NOSE!*

I have low blood pressure, and once my husband had to call the paramedics because it bottomed out on me. One of the paramedics turned out to be my former student. I was sitting there in my second-rattiest bra with my "boats and hoes" T-shirt pulled up over my bra so he could put the sticker things on me, feeling like I was both about to die and die of embarrassment. Then, I KID YOU NOT, my precious, darling children surveyed the situation and the oldest one said, "This means I can miss school tomorrow, right?" And the second-oldest one said, "Can I get another cookie?"

Anson: *I can run away from my shadow because I am THAT fast.* [As someone who has chased him up and down the valley we live in, I can attest to the fact that he is quite fast.]

While pulling in a parking lot, a truck in front of me was taking its sweet time to park, so I sighed impatiently and said, "MOVE, YOU'RE IN MY WAY" in the privacy of my own car. Then, of course, we got out at the same time as they were getting out of their truck. Anson looked at them and loudly said, "There's the people that were in your way, Mom!"

We were at our favorite donut shop one morning and Anson asked for money to put in the tip jar. I didn't have any cash (I left a tip on the card, don't worry!), so I said, "I don't have any money." And that kid looked me dead in the eyes, lowered his voice, and said, "You can steal money from banks." And I thought, "My God, I bet he's going to do that one day."

We once took the kids to the Ark Encounter when Avery was six. Avery was so excited the night before we went he couldn't stop asking questions.

Avery: *Is Noah gonna be there?*
Me: *No.*
Avery: *Noah isn't with his own ark?*
Me: *Noah's dead.*
Avery: *But his ark is alive?*
Me: *Yes. Wait, no. Arks aren't alive.*
Avery: *What kind of motor does the ark have?*
Me: *No motor.*
Avery: *How did it run, then?*
Me: [sighs] *I don't know. Miracle.*
Avery: *How deep is the water gonna be?*
Me: *No water. Just the ark.*
Avery: *No flood? Then how is it floating?*
Me: *It's not. It's just sitting.*

Avery: *Sitting where? On what?*
Me: *Um, right where God wants it, I guess.*
Avery: *Oh, so is God gonna be there?*
Me: *No.*
Avery: *But you've said before that God is everywhere.*
Me: ….
Avery: *So is He?*
Me: *IDK, GO TO SLEEP.*

One morning, my husband told Anson they were going to go fishing that afternoon. (He fell in TWICE the previous time they went.) When he got the news, he closed his eyes and started chanting to himself, "I am NOT going to fall in today. I am NOT going to fall in today."

This is a photo of Anson, age one, at a graveside funeral, in January. He got away from me and ran into a pond in subfreezing temperatures. Guess who got to wade in and retrieve him?

Anson: steals the baby's pacifier
My mom: *Anson, why in the world would you take a baby's*

pacifier?

Anson: *She owes me money.*

Anson: *Mom! I found you something!* [hands me a dead lizard]

I once stopped at Hobby Lobby to grab some stuff and had Anson with me. Anson kept asking the name of the store, but couldn't remember it. All he could remember was that it was two words that rhymed. So then he would say stuff like, "When can we go back to Poppy Toppy?" and "I had fun at Duppy Wuppy."

Anson: *Mommy, what does your shirt say?*
Me: *It says, "Oh play me some mountain music."*
Anson: *It can't say that ... There is NEVER any music on the mountains.*

Us, his parents: *Anson, always do your best on your schoolwork, even the simple things.*
Anson: *Nope.*

❖ ❖ ❖

Anson: *Can we eat at a food house?*
Me: *.... Do you mean a restaurant?*
Anson: *Yes, a food house. A place with all the food.*

❖ ❖ ❖

Driving home from the sitter with Anson one afternoon, he said, "I love you" from the backseat. And naturally I said, "I love you too!" But then he said, "I WAS TALKING TO MYSELF."

❖ ❖ ❖

I had to take Anson to a pre-kindergarten screening when he was four. They quizzed him on basic vocabulary by showing him photos of common objects (window, sock, hat, etc.). Then they held up a feather. My little founding father thought for a second and then said, with gusto, that it was a quill pen.

◆ ◆ ◆

Parenting is so weird—I had to rearrange my whole day and leave the baby with a sitter just to go to "field day" and watch Avery (middle left) pull on this rope for about 40 seconds.

◆ ◆ ◆

Anson: sneezes, doesn't cover his mouth, it goes everywhere, including all over my lap and my lunch
Anson: *Did you see that, Mom? It was like a METEOR SHOWER!*

◆ ◆ ◆

Avery, June 10, 5:43 a.m.: *Mom? Mom? MOM? Can I tell you what I want for Christmas now?*

◆ ◆ ◆

If you have kids, you know they always have to potty at terrible times. Well, once we were on the road to Tybee Island, which is desolate, and Anson had to go. I said, "Well, sorry, buddy. You'll have to hold it for a few minutes." So we were driving along and Avery said, "Wow! That house is beautiful!" And Anson said, "YEAH, SO BEAUTIFUL. SURE WISH I COULD POOP IN IT."

Anson went through a phase where he wouldn't tell me he loved me, but he had no problem saying, "I love you so much!" to my mom's neighbor's dog every time he saw it.

Anson once cried for what felt like forever because he couldn't find his homework. He was four and had never in his life had homework.

My husband was a groomsman in a fancy wedding once when Avery was four. During the reception, we had an African-American waitress who was taking plates and refilling drinks. She looked at Avery and smiled. He smiled back and said, "Hey, so why are you black?"

There was a farm day event at Anson's preschool one day, and a farmer let the kids make butter in a little ramekin to bring home. Anson was so proud of his butter; he carried it around all weekend (gross, I know). He used it as punishment for anyone in the house who wronged him: "If you don't stop that, you can't see my butter!" I can't even begin to explain to you the mom guilt I felt when I had to throw away the unrefrigerated butter.

We watched the "Madagascar" movies in the car on the way to our vacation destination once. The oldest two thought it was so funny to mimic King Julien's accent all week long, which I'm sure was SUPER-OFFENSIVE to the lovely Indian couple who owned the hotel where we stayed.

◆ ◆ ◆

Upon rescuing an earthworm from the pavement and putting it back in the grass, Avery (about three at the time) said, "Bye, worm! Tell your mama I said hi!"

◆ ◆ ◆

I left the room for one minute; I returned to the room to find the baby had climbed onto the table, opened a bag of chips, dumped one bag of chips, and was eating another bag of chips. One. Minute.

I took the boys to a waterpark one summer, and in true "too old for young fun" fashion, I hurt my tailbone on a waterslide. And I mean I HURT it. I limped around for several days, and bending over was awful. During the midst of this injury, I took the boys school shopping, and as I struggled to bend over to get something out of a bin, Avery loudly proclaimed, as he saw me struggling to get up, "IS YOUR BUTT STILL HURTING, MOM?"

Me: *Avery, go put on your jammies.*
Avery: *THIS HOUSE IS A PRISON.*

I'm sorry for all of you parents who hate to see summer break ending, but by the end of one summer, Avery was literally in the living room LOUDLY stabbing a cardboard box with a pair of scissors because he was "SO BORED," only stopping periodically to ask me things like "Were there toilets on the ark?" and "Will there be Godzillas in heaven?" I would have given anyone without a prison record $6,000 to get him out of my house.

Once when Anson was two, we got a coupon in the mail, ADDRESSED TO HIM, from Craft Beer Club. It's a mystery we still haven't solved.

Here's some cute neologisms my children used at one point or another:
  -Squishy pants (sweatpants)
  -Abobobobo (hippopotamus—it's like he wouldn't even try the actual pronunciation)
  -Granny crackers (graham crackers)
  -Ramen noodles (pool noodles)
  -Bargoog (garbage)
  -Zebras (flamingos, and vice versa)
  -Jumpoline (trampoline)
  -Motorbikle (motorcycle)
  -Crocodickle (crocodile)
  -Hoopball (basketball)
  -Spoofbrush (toothbrush)

Avery went through a phase where he would bid people goodbye by telling them to "stay handsome."
Me: *Bye, Avery!*
Avery: *Stay handsome, Mom!*

Me: *OK .... I'll try?*

Anson is usually an incredibly smart child, but he once did something that made me change my mind a little. He invented a game called Pancakes. Apparently both players (he and Archer) started with a stack of [imaginary] pancakes. But then Archer stole some of the pancakes (Archer had no idea he did this, by the way). Anson was unable to make more because he "didn't have a pancake machine." So he cried for 20 minutes about missing pancakes he never had to start with. They played this game often and someone always ended up crying. My husband and I ultimately had to forbid Pancakes.

Avery: *What happens if you punch a penguin?*

As I was taking Anson to the sitter's one morning, I had to slam on my brakes because a wild turkey (or some other large bird) ran into the road. This made Anson drop his donut (it was still in the bag, so the donut was fine). But still, Anson yelled, "OHHH THAT BIRD MADE ME DROP MY DONUT; I HATE THAT BIRD FOREVER."

Once at the grocery store, my child asked for some overpriced sugary cereal and I said no. He let it go and didn't say anything else about it—until we got to the register with lots of people around. He LOUDLY started crying and saying he wished we could afford all the food we needed. I'm honestly a little shocked no one offered me grocery money after his performance.

◆ ◆ ◆

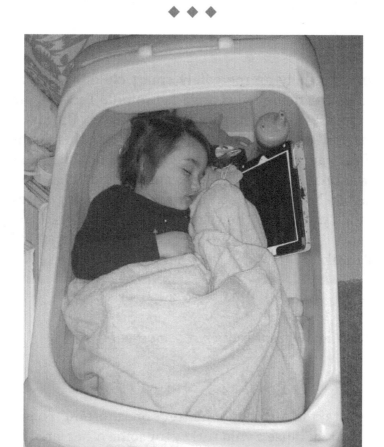

When we bought this plastic toy chest for the garage, Avery was so excited about it he wanted to sleep in it. So I dragged it in the house, made him a little soft nest in it, and let him sleep. How did he thank me? By going to Sunday school the next morning and telling his teacher I made him sleep in a hard box all night.

Avery: *If you have six people in your family, how many pounds is*

that? Of garbage?

When kindergarten started, we had a talk with Avery about how we had to do everything our teacher said. So after he got in the car after his first day, Avery said, "Mrs. Melanie said we had to go to the store and get any toy I want this weekend." Nice try, kid.

Avery: *What did Anson do while I was at school today?*
Me: *Ate. Played. Created chaos. Almost pulled Grandma's TV down on himself.*
Avery: *Did he break it?*
Me: *No. But if it had fallen on him, he'd have gotten smushed.*
Avery: *Dang, that would've been cool if he died.*

Anson, waking me from a nap with hysterical tears: *Mom, Avery said there were cupcakes and THERE ARE NO CUPCAKES.*

How a child could possibly get the chocolate muffin he ate for breakfast in multiple stains down the BACK of his shirt is surely going to be looked into on a future season of "Unsolved Mysteries."

Before my middle son was potty trained, he used to love to sit on the front porch in his diaper. This would've been much cuter, of course, if it wasn't the neighbor's porch he was so fond of sitting on. (You can barely see him in this photo, but that's him in the circle, just trespassing and relaxing.)

I once left Anson in his high chair while I took Avery to the bathroom. While we were gone, he managed to wiggle his way to a KNIFE left on the kitchen counter and THROW IT into the floor, where it went into the hardwood and stood straight up. I came back to a scene straight out of a horror movie with a knife standing straight up in front of Chucky (I mean Anson). But the baby was unhurt (can't say the same for the hardwood floors). The next day, Anson woke up sick and I had to take him to a clinic. Avery, quite the chatterbox then and now, was with us. When the nurse practitioner asked me what was wrong, Avery butted in before I could answer to say, "Oh, he was just playing with a knife." He also told the NP how Anson nearly choked to death on a leaf he insisted on trying to eat a couple of weeks before that (also true).

If your child, like mine, has a Croc obsession, do NOT accidentally put one in the dryer. Trust me.

Anson was munching on a plate of carrots and ranch. I walked by when he was done and noticed the plate looked spotless with no trace of ranch. I said, "Anson, did you LICK the leftover ranch off your plate?" And he said," Sure did, bro" and licked the plate again for good measure. He was four.

During a snowstorm when we were snowed in, things really took a dark turn after about four days of seeing no one but each other. The oldest two kids started trading "yo mama" insults, which I found greatly offensive. Then, Avery started eating nacho cheese by itself with a spoon, as though it was pudding or yogurt, and all the kids cried when we ran out of nacho cheese.

Trying to pep talk Archer into being nice on the way to school during one of his mean phases:
Me: *Are you Mommy's best boy?*
Archer: *Yeah!*
Me: *Are you my handsome boy?*
Archer: *Yeah!*
Me: *Are you gonna be so good today?*
Archer: *Ye*— [realizes he's been tricked and shuts up]

Anson, one lovely spring afternoon: "Mom, I had the best day at school. I found a marshmallow and I ate it!" The next morning, he was like, "Man, that marshmallow was good. Marshmallows make you strong! I can't believe I found a marshmallow!" No one could be happier about finding Atlantis than he was about the marshmallow—even though his daycare teacher informed me there had been no marshmallows in the building since December, so it must've been *one stale marshmallow.*

The woman who owns the donut shop in our town is used to seeing my kids all the time, and always gives them hugs and kisses. I almost died of embarrassment when Avery (age four) returned her affection by smacking her on the butt.

I was about two days away from giving birth to Ada when I took this picture, so bending over was *the worst.*

Me: *Ugh, Archer, did you make a mess?*

Archer: nods proudly and vigorously

When Anson was a little over a year old, we went to a zoo where you could have a "kangaroo experience" and go into their enclosure. We were there on the verge of a thunderstorm, and it was pouring rain. These kangaroos were already *over it.* Since we had already paid the admission despite the rain, we went inside with them anyway. Anson picked up a stick. When I tell you before I could BLINK we were surrounded by a pack of kangaroos ready to fight, I am not exaggerating. Apparently, picking up that stick was a sign of deep offense (or aggression, probably) to the kangaroo community. I was pregnant with my third child, but I still had to gather my existing children, one under each arm, and drag them out of that pen before we became an unfortunate kangaroo fatality statistic.

◆ ◆ ◆

On our way to pre-K one morning, Anson stopped to grab not one snack, but two. Then when he opened his lunchbox to put them inside, I saw he had already packed another snack. I said, "Anson, why in the world do you need three snacks?" And he said, "Mom, I need provisions" dead-serious, like he was setting out on the Oregon Trail and not headed to preschool with his Sonic the Hedgehog backpack.

◆ ◆ ◆

Avery was in kindergarten when Archer was born, and he was so proud to have a new sibling (don't worry, it faded) at first. So proud, in fact, that he must have been bragging to his friends, because one day he came home with a baby gift for Archer— a onesie with the name "Stella Rose" on it. Evidently, it had belonged to a friend of his when she was a baby, and her mom had been hanging on to it all those years. Avery refused to return it to Stella ("That would be rude, Mommy!"), so I had to take it to the elementary school office for them to get it back to Stella's mom.

Guy at McDonald's drive-thru: *Thank you, please pull around.*
Anson: *OK, I LOVE YOU!*

Avery got invited to a party at a friend's home once, and we made the regretful decision of taking Anson, too. Here's a list of things he did during our hour there before we gave up and left before we were asked to leave:

-got himself locked in a chicken coop filled with roosters (he's super-lucky he didn't get flogged to death before I got there)

-let one of the said roosters escape (I didn't SEE him do this, but I felt confident he was the perpetrator)

-hit someone's cat with a bubble wand

-poured said cat's water out and gave the cat Sprite instead

-stuck his hands in a cake that was in no way, shape, or form meant for him

-put a cigarette butt he found on the ground in his mouth

-also found a lighter that accompanied the cigarette butt and was pretty close to burning his fingers before I got it away from him

-pushed a kid down who wouldn't share his candy with him

-managed to get Tootsee Roll stuck in his hair, which had to be cut out

The kids usually sit on my bed while I'm in the master bath getting ready in the mornings so I can at least hear what they are up to even if I can't see them. One morning, I heard Avery telling

Anson how some skin colors are cooler than others. When I tell you my heart broke …. I slung that bathroom door open and went out there to correct my little racists right then and there …. only to find them comparing shades of green on their Ninja Turtle toys. PHEWWWW.

◆ ◆ ◆

One morning as I was getting the kids ready and buckled in the car, I ran back inside to grab my coffee. When I turned around, Anson was standing there eating a chocolate donut. We didn't have any chocolate donuts in the house. I still have no idea where he got this.

I once bought a bottle of Torani syrup at TJ Maxx because I was excited to find sugar-free white chocolate. An added motive for this purchase was that I had a subpar cup of coffee waiting in the car that could use some flavor. So I got to the parking lot, loaded Ada (a newborn at the time) in the car, then cracked the syrup open and poured some in my cup. As I turned my head to back out, I noticed there was a woman in the car next to me watching in abject horror. I realized pretty quickly that she thought I'd just poured a shot of alcohol into my coffee and was about to drink and drive, with a newborn in tow. I'm honestly kind of surprised she didn't call the police, but if she did, they did not find me. Avery also once (loudly, at the register, where hecould humiliate me in front of the maximum number of people) begged me to "stop buying alcohol" when I purchased some Torani syrup. The moral of this story is that Torani needs to reconsider the shape of their bottles.

Here's a story that illustrates my kids' eating habits pretty well: I took them out to eat and ordered them both something I was sure they'd love. Avery wouldn't even try his and only ate chips. Anson ate all of his, all of Avery's, and—before I could stop him— a french fry he picked up off the ground in the parking lot on our way to the car. (In fact, if I had a dollar for all the parking lot fries this child has eaten over the course of his existence ....)

I once overheard my kid say to another kid on the playground, "My daddy has a nice boat. It's not a mean boat."

Avery: *I'm gonna own a lemonade stand when I grow up. Seems like an easy way to get rich.*

If there's one thing my kids excel at, it's getting stuck. Here's one of them stuck under the crib and another one stuck in a doll-size shopping cart.

The only thing more exhausting than being pregnant is being pregnant and having other toddlers in the home. One afternoon during my last couple of weeks of pregnancy with Ada, I felt as though I was about to fall down. The two middle kids were at daycare, so I told Avery (age seven) to watch his iPad while I took a nap and to not wake me unless there was an emergency. But his Nerf gun jammed about 20 minutes into my nap, so naturally that was an emergency.

I once had to dig through the trash for my youngest son when he was two years old. He was crying inconsolably because I had thrown away a prized possession of his. That possession was a used Band-Aid.

Anson might have a future career in politics. After being mean as a snake all morning, we went into a gas station in South Georgia for a snack while we were on vacation. He inexplicably began singing "Jesus Loves Me." Loudly. And he sang it with a few of the words he knew wrong or missing for extra little kid cuteness. People were oohing and awwing and telling me how sweet he was. I swear I saw someone filming (send it to me if you see it on TikTok). He was working it like Missy Elliot in her 2002 video of the same name. Then he finished and smiled at me (and I swear he would've winked if he knew how) and went right on back to the car and being the little jerk he usually is.

Archer got car sick in Atlanta on the way to vacation once. But me being the super-mom I am, I was ready with a bag! Yay me! Well, by the time I crossed 204 lanes of traffic to pull over, the bottom had fallen out of that bag and puke was everywhere. The car smelled awful, and the other kids were gagging. My father-in-law and I stripped him naked on I-75 and changed his clothes, but there wasn't much we could do for the car seat. I wiped it down the best I could, but that smell stuck with us all the way to the hotel (by the way, if you've never disassembled a car seat in a hotel parking lot and then scrubbed it in a hotel bathtub, then congratulations, your life is going better than mine). But Archer wasn't done torturing us yet. The next day, we were walking downtown, and there was a puddle that was obviously, by both look and smell, contaminated with human feces. Archer has a pair of rain boots he LOVES and wears all the time, but was he wearing them this day? Oh no. Despite me SCREAMING at him to stop, he ran right through this ankle-deep puddle while all the people around us gasped in horror and looked at me for my response. I considered leaving him behind, but there were too many witnesses. So I pulled out my phone and found out there was a Baby Gap a few blocks away. We started walking. Guys, when I say he stank, I mean he STANK. People were GAGGING as we passed. Kids were saying, "Mom! What IS THAT SMELL?" He was wet almost up to his knees as the liquid crept upward by the time we got there, but he seemed blissfully unaware that he smelled like actual crap. I had to buy new pants, shoes, and socks in Gap, and scrub his feet/legs the best I could with a pack of baby wipes I paid *$6.99* for at a tourist trap store. I double-bagged the clothes to bring them home to wash, but the car still smelled like sewage and puke for the rest of the trip.

Once while on THE SAME TRIP, we encountered a large group of tourists who were taking up the whole sidewalk. They were slightly inebriated and having a good time, and genuinely didn't realize they were in the way. I said, "Excuse me" and got no response; then my father-in-law said, "Excuse me" and got no response. So Anson shouted "MOVVVEEEEEEEEEEEE" at the absolute top of his lungs and they parted like the Red Sea. Some chuckled and some looked at me like I was the worst parent in the world as my family and I passed through the group with our heads hung down in shame.

Our oldest went through a phase where he said, "Oh no!" a lot, but he didn't understand what context to use it in. Examples include:

-"OH NOOOOO, cows say moo."

-"OH NOOOOO, Mommy has TWO EYES."
-"OH NOOOOO, that's a red fire truck."

My husband was on a stepladder in the kitchen helping me get down the Christmas dishes one peaceful November afternoon (they're in that useless cabinet everyone has in their kitchen that's too high to reach for everyday items) while the boys were sitting at the table eating pizza. Ada, who had already eaten, was sitting under the table begging for scraps, like a dog. Suddenly, Anson gagged (this is not unusual, as Anson throws up more than any child I've ever known or known of), but when it's a serious gag, he usually makes it to the bathroom. But not this day, oh no. He threw up all over the table and the chair he was sitting in, plus down the front of himself. He hopped up like he was going to head to the bathroom, but another wave hit him, and he threw up ALLLLLL over the only path out of the kitchen. This all happened so fast Ash hadn't even descended the ladder. Before he could even get one step down, Ada had made her way out from under the table and crawled through the puke. Ash, off the ladder by this point, had just pole-vaulted over the giant puddle of vomit and grabbed Ada when Anson threw up some more. All this time Archer had been handling things well, but then the smell got to him and he started gagging, too. I have never moved so fast as I did to get that boy to the trash can (thank God we made it) because I could NOT handle two puddles that size. Meanwhile, Anson was still spewing like a fountain and at one point even turned his head and sprayed some down the cabinets and across the countertop. Archer and I were trapped behind the puddle, which was growing by the second, with no way out of the kitchen. Ash had already headed to the bathroom with Ada to start some bath water when Archer decided he'd also try to jump over the puddle. He didn't make it over, OF COURSE, and he SLIPPED AND FELL IN IT. So then he was gagging some more, crying because he's covered in puke, and Ash and I were just overcome by giggles because of the insanity of it all. I had to tiptoe through it to get out of the kitchen and to the towels because, believe it or not, I'm not a great distance jumper. We had bathed all three of them, got them dressed in pajamas, and headed to the kitchen for work that we really should've hired a HAZMAT crew to do when Anson came in crying because he got a monster truck toy stuck in his hair. (He refuses to get a haircut because he's afraid it will hurt.) I had to make him hang out with his hair tangled in a truck for a while because I was still in the middle of the last problem he had caused. We finally got the kitchen cleaned, the truck removed, and were getting back to the Christmas task at hand when Anson declared, "I'm never going to eat again," and then, I kid you not, within the same minute said, "Can I have some cookies?"

The next morning, the first thing Anson said to me when he got up was, "Mom, remember when I threw up everywhere yesterday?" As though that image won't haunt me for all my days, and likely be the last thought I have as I'm leaving this plane of existence.

Yes, son, please get a toy tangled in your hair while your father and I are busy shoveling your puke into the garbage can.

This paper towel pile represents the size of the puke puddle.

Really? You can only think of ONE thing in the entire world you're thankful for, kid? And Funyuns, for real? Not even cheddar and sour cream Ruffles, which is clearly a superior chip?

❖ ❖ ❖

If you don't already know this, don't ever let your children sense how excited you are about an item of food, because the more excited you are to eat it, the more likely they are to sneeze in it.

❖ ❖ ❖

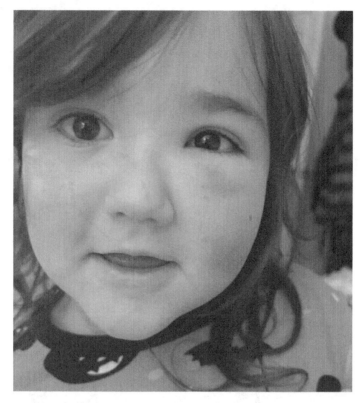

I was trying to hold Anson back from running away from me one time, but I failed. He broke free, but the momentum of it caused him to spring forward and fall, which ultimately caused the whole left side of his face to turn blue. All I could think of when I looked at him during that time was Mel Gibson's face painted blue in "Braveheart" and his cry of "FREEDOM," which is what Anson wanted when he fell.

There are nights that Anson decides he only wants a lemon for dinner. We also once paid $6.99 at a Chinese buffet for him to eat nothing but four lemon wedges. (He also once threw up on the carpet at that same Chinese restaurant. I *know* they hate to see us coming.)

◆ ◆ ◆

Avery: *MOM, ANSON IS BEING A TURD!*
Me: *Listen, you're not wrong, but let's not say "turd," OK?*
I can't believe no one has ever asked me to teach parenting classes since I regularly give this kind of top-notch advice.

◆ ◆ ◆

The actual second I got him out of the car on River Street, Savannah, Georgia's most crowded tourist area, he dropped his pants.

The rest of Anson's team

Anson

Made the mistake of signing Anson up for soccer one year. He didn't last.

Once while on vacation, we visited a military museum and the curator asked, "Is anyone here in the military?" And Anson, four at the time, loudly said, "YES, I AM IN THE LORD'S ARMY." (He got a free patch!)

Once when getting the kids ready to go see Santa, I asked Archer what he wanted for Christmas. He sighed deeply and said, "To sit down."

Me too, buddy.

When the COVID shutdown began, we explained to Avery we wouldn't be leaving the house without wearing masks anymore, so he ran to his toy box and, well, let's just say there was a misunderstanding over the type of mask we meant.

◆ ◆ ◆

I will never understand why someone's crack is always showing. Don't they feel a breeze?

◆ ◆ ◆

Sometimes when Avery was little, he'd assume such a serious demeanor and position that I thought he was about to scold me about 401(k) distributions.

Just standing outside in his diaper eating stale bread out of the birdfeeder, like no one ever gave him anything fresh to eat inside the actual house.

My mom acts a tad dramatic when I'm driving and grabs the bar above the window every time I hit my brakes. There was a time when Avery was small that he began to think that's what you were supposed to do when someone hit their brakes, and he never missed grabbing it when someone slowed down.

I understand why he didn't want to nap with pants on. But I've never figured out why he was fine with leaving his shoes on. This habit of removing pants, keeping shoes to sleep continued until he was almost five.

One morning, while on a trip, as we were leaving our hotel, Anson held the door for our family and then continued holding the door for what was very obviously a female behind us. She thanked him with a big smile and I said, "Anson! That was so nice of you to hold the door for us and then a stranger too!" And he said, clearly still within her earshot, "YEAH, I THOUGHT IT WOULD BE NICE TO HOLD THE DOOR FOR THAT MAN."

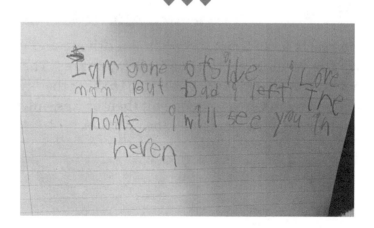

Avery and Anson got in big trouble one night and Daddy yelled at them (which is rare and really hurts their feelings). Avery said he was going to run away from home and, being the stellar parent I am, I said, "OK I'll get the door for you." So he "ran away" (he sat on the porch for four minutes—the boy didn't even put shoes on) and left this super-dramatic note behind: "See you in heven."

Anson, ever the stubborn child, went through a time where he would not leave his coat on. This caused anarchy at daycare with all the other kids wanting to rip their coats off, too. So his teacher started zipping his coat on him backward, hood in his face.

When they first discovered temporary tattoos, I had to, at their insistence, add "tattoo the kids every morning" to my long list of things to do before 7 a.m.

◆ ◆ ◆

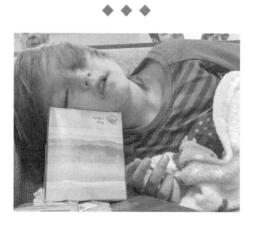

Some kids, like my second born, are TERRIBLE sleepers who struggle to rest in even the most comfortable of conditions. Others, like my oldest, can literally fall asleep on a Kleenex box during a church sermon.

◆ ◆ ◆

Ada rarely sleeps without smushing something up to her face. Once while I was putting away laundry and she was near my laundry pile, she grabbed a pair of her brother's underwear and cuddled up to take a nap. Thank goodness they were from the clean pile.

◆ ◆ ◆

My husband and I wildly inconvenienced ourselves one Easter weekend to take the kids to an Easter egg hunt and party at a nearby church. But, for whatever reason, a couple of our kids had absolute nervous breakdowns that forced us to drag half of them out screaming, kicking, and crying during the telling of the Easter story. Once back home, Archer, one of the meltdowners, had what appeared to be a marvelous time watching clothes tumble in the dryer. Obviously we should have skipped the inconvenience and stayed home to start with. Kids are so weird.

Driving through a neighboring town, one of the boys had to pee. No problem, he's a boy! We'll just pull in at the park and let him go around to the side of the car for privacy. Except he didn't go around to the side of the car for privacy—he just dropped his pants right on the town's main thoroughfare, mere inches from their "welcome to our town" sign, and provided a free show to passersby that, had he been 15 years older, would've gotten him arrested and on a sex offender list.

After trick-or-treating one year, we went to a local church that was providing free nachos for dinner. The kids were opening their treat bags, and Anson found he had gotten a bouncy ball in one of his bags. Avery, being mean, took a swipe at it, and Anson screamed, *at this church event*, "MOM, AVERY FLICKED MY BALL!"

Not our kid having to be forced back into his pants after taking them off in McDonald's so he could eat his fries sans britches, as the Lord intended.

My kids love the Christmas movie "Elf," so we watch it on repeat throughout November and December. I think the whole movie lives rent-free in their heads year-round. There's that scene where the narwhal says, as he's leaving the North Pole, "Bye, Buddy! I hope you find your dad!" ... Anyway, one summer afternoon, months away from "Elf" season, I was driving along a backroad with Anson and spotted a turtle. I pulled over and got Anson out for a learning opportunity, telling him how to carry turtles to the other side of the road so they don't get run over and cautioning him about not removing them from the immediate area they are in. I picked the turtle up carefully and addressed it as "buddy" when I did so. When I released it on the other side, Anson said, "Bye, Buddy! I hope you find your dad!"

Avery (age three): *My hands are grouchy.*

Avery, the night of the 2024 presidential election: *Who is winning the presidential race?*
Anson: *I'm in sixth place.*

Someone ran over the mailbox at King Donuts, our favorite donut shop, and didn't stop. A police officer tracked them down, but they had no insurance and expressed no intention to pay for the mailbox replacement. The owner told me this story one morning, and I relayed it to Avery. He said, "I HOPE THAT DRIVER GETS THE DEATH PENALTY."

One year during our first "Elf" viewing of the holiday season, Avery had *lots* of questions about the gift that Buddy buys "for that special someone" (a set of Santa-themed lingerie, in case you've not seen the movie). He asked me what it was and I told him it was underwear. And he said, "My underwear doesn't look like that!" And so I said, "Well, it's girl underwear." And he said, "Your underwear doesn't look like that!" And I said, "Well, it's underwear you would only wear in front of one other person." And he said, "Ewwww, why? Who would you wear that in front of, Mom?" And that's where I gave up trying to answer his questions about lingerie.

Anson (unintentionally) pretending he's a Homer Simpson GIF

Archer, shaking a bottled Coke Zero:
My husband: *NOOO, don't shake those!*
Anson: *What happens if you shake one?*
My husband: (knowing if he told Anson they explode that Anson would try it): *YOU GO TO PRISON.*

At church:
"Let us pray. Dear Heavenly Father, we thank you f—"
Anson: *I CAN SPELL ELEPHANT!*
On the way home from church:
"Mom, how do you spell 'bra'?"
"Does G-A-Y spell Jameson?"

We drove by US Xpress (a trucking company) headquarters one day, and its interesting shape caught Anson's eye. I told him I used to work there. "What's it like inside?" he asked. "Like what color are the toilets?"

Anson is very curious about measurements. One day he asked me, "Mom, how high are you?" I stared at him blankly (though I wasn't high at all) until I realized he was asking me my height.

Anson, inventing a game:
"You throw it three times and if you get it in all three times you win! And if you miss you lose. And then you have to go to Korea."
(His dad chimed in with, "North or South?")

Me: *Mom, Anson skinned his nose. Can you put some cream on it?* [I meant Neosporin.]
Mom: slathers my child's face in Ben Gay

Every morning after brushing his teeth, Anson asks, "Does my breath look good?"

When Anson was three, he got a case of RSV and I had to take him to a walk-in clinic. He is unruly at doctors' offices in the best of conditions, but when he's also sick and not feeling like being messed with, it's next level. After they weighed him, which was an ordeal in itself, he broke free of me and ran into an exam room, where he wedged himself so tightly under the table that a doctor, three nurses, and myself had to physically move the table to extract him. I'm shocked we weren't asked to leave, but I have definitely been ashamed to take him back.

Anson: *So is Santa coming tonight while we sleep?* [he had Santa on his mind because we had gone to see him that morning]

Me: *No, it's not Christmas Eve.*

Anson: *So today is .... false Christmas?*

November 16 will henceforth be known as False Christmas in our home.

Me: *Avery, go brush your teeth!*

Avery: *My pants are uncomfortable!* [All my pants are uncomfortable, kid. Get used to it.]

My husband: *That doesn't mean you don't have to brush your teeth.*

Avery, bursting into tears: *I KNEW I WASN'T LOVED!*

Anson was once playing in a laundry basket I had sitting on the bed, and he somehow rocked it so far to the edge it slid off and became wedged between the bed and crib (see his hand sticking out in the circled portion above?). Anson weighed about 30 pounds at the time, and I *almost never* got him dislodged from this scenario. I thought I was going to have to call the fire department for assistance.

Even from a young age, one of Anson's favorite pastimes was thumbing through food magazines.

This photo captures the moment that Anson learned the absolute decadence of dipping his roll in his mashed potatoes.

In kindergarten, Avery was given this "words I like" activity. There are lots of things I like about it, but my favorite thing is how he accidentally wrote "beer" before correcting it to "deer."

◆ ◆ ◆

One final (there have been SO many in his short existence) "I lost Anson" story: We went on a small vacation to the Birmingham Zoo one summer. My father-in-law was with us, as he usually is on vacation, to help out with the children. Even with three adults supervising, we looked up to find Anson was missing. My father-in-law ran one way, my husband ran another, and I stayed put with the other kids in case he came back to our last known location. Minutes passed. He goes missing so often I didn't panic at first, but after 20 minutes of no word from my FIL or my husband, I was truly worried. I made the others jump in our wagon so I could rapidly head to the front of the zoo to make sure no one was trying to leave with him (they'd be sorry because he never sleeps and eats $20 in groceries a day, but they might not have known they made a bad kidnapping choice until it was too late). I ran into my husband, also clearly panicked, on the way. We decided the time had come to tell security. As we entered the gift shop to ask them to get us some help, we saw him—just standing there looking at merchandise like he had both good sense and a credit card. My husband yelled at him so loudly for this infraction that Anson *still* apologizes about it once a week or so.

To the family walking their kid by to see our Christmas decorations at the same moment my husband stepped onto the porch in his underwear and "Ernest Scared Stupid" T-shirt to yell at Archer to "GET YOUR BUTT IN THE HOUSE" .... we are so sorry; please consider this your public apology.

ABOUT THE AUTHOR

Ashley L. Hall

 Ashley is a former college instructor, a freelance editor and writer, an Etsy shop owner, and a legal research assistant. In her free time, whatever that is, she enjoys reading, watching true crime TV and horror movies, perusing thrift stores, and decorating (and redecorating ad nauseum). She and her husband met in middle school but did not become a couple until much later. They married in 2013 and welcomed their first child in 2016.

Made in United States
Cleveland, OH
03 January 2025

12877483R10066